TIME OF
BURNING

TIME OF BURNING

B. Davie Napier

Pilgrim Press
Philadelphia   Boston

SBN 8298-0156-1

Library of Congress Catalog Card Number 74-117723

To students

at Stanford University,

who have been my teachers

since 1966

CONTENTS

PART 2

THE BURNING
IN THE TEMPLE

Introduction to and verses from Isaiah 6   32

PART 3

THE BURNING
IN THE BONES

Verses from Jeremiah 1, 20, and 8   52

PART 4

THE BURNING
IN GOD AND MAN

Verses from Jonah and the Gospels   72

INTRODUCTION

Some readers will be familiar with the form of "the burnings" from my earlier contemporizing interpretations of five Genesis stories in *Come Sweet Death*. Every generation continues to read with immediate meaning the varied stuff of biblical literature because it never simply "was" but always "is."

This is a quartet from the Prophets, a free, present-tense reading of narratives about three real men and one just as real but not historical, not in the realm of facticity—Moses, Isaiah, Jeremiah, and Jonah. These readings are free and contemporary in the sense that I have taken the liberty of putting us into them.

This quartet first saw the light of day, or better, first knew its own sound, as sermons in University Public Worship at Stanford during the winter and spring of 1969. Three of the quartet were the basis of worship services at the annual Pastors' Conference and Earl Lectures at Pacific School of Religion in Berkeley in 1969. Individual units, or parts of the quartet, have been read at Rice, Vanderbilt, Washington University, Yale, and other colleges and universities. The entire quartet was spoken as sermons during the meeting of the General Synod of the United Church of Christ in the summer of 1969.

I am as always indebted to my wife, Joy, a sensitive, discerning, but ultimately supportive critic. Stanford students, to whom this volume is dedicated, have been for several years now not only members of my congregation and of my classes, but at the same time my gentle guides into the prophetic perspectives of their generation. They are emphatically more closely kin to the Old Testament prophets than any of those who have gone before them. And to that fabulous company who produced the whole Old Testament prophetic "mind" I am and will be to my death inexpressibly grateful.

Davie Napier
Stanford University, California

PART 1

THE BURNING
IN THE MIDST

Verses from Exodus 1-4

1:1 ff. These came to Egypt with Jacob, seventy persons. Joseph was already in Egypt. Then Joseph died, and all his brothers, and all that generation. But the descendants of Israel were fruitful and increased greatly; they multiplied and grew exceedingly strong; so that the land was filled with them.

Now there arose a new king over Egypt who did not know Joseph.

"Look," Pharaoh said to his people, "these people, the sons of Israel, have become so numerous and strong that they are a threat to us. We must be prudent. If war should break out, they might add to the number of our enemies. They might escape out of the country." Accordingly, the Egyptians forced the sons of Israel into slavery, and made their lives unbearable with hard labor, work with clay and with brick, and with all kinds of work in the fields.

3:1 ff. Now Moses led his flock to Horeb, the mountain of God. And lo, a bush was burning yet it was not consumed. And Moses said, "I will turn aside and see this great sight, why the bush is not burnt." And God called to him from the midst of the bush, "Moses, Moses!" And he said, "Here am I." Then God said, "Put off your shoes from your feet, for the place on which you are standing is holy ground."

3:10 ff. God said to Moses, "Come, I will send you to Pharaoh that you may bring my people out of Egypt." But Moses said, "Who am I, that I should go? . . .

4:1 ff. "They will not believe me." The Lord said to him, "What is that in your hand?" He said, "A staff." "Throw it on the ground," the Lord said. So he threw it on the ground, and it turned into a serpent. "Put out your hand and catch it by the tail," and in his hand the serpent turned into a staff. "Put your hand into your bosom," and when he drew it out, his hand was covered with leprosy, white as snow. "Put your hand back into your bosom." He did; and when he drew it out, there it was restored. "But if they should believe neither of these two signs, you must take water from the river and pour it on the ground; and the water you have drawn from the river will turn to blood on the ground."

4:10 ff. Moses said to the Lord, "But, my Lord, never in my life have I been a man of eloquence, either before or since you have spoken to your servant. I am a slow speaker and not able to speak well." "Who gave man his mouth?" the Lord answered him. "Who makes him dumb or deaf, gives him sight or leaves him blind? Is it not I? Now go, I shall help you to speak and tell you what to say."

I

Exodus
1:1 ff. *These came to Egypt with Jacob, seventy persons. Joseph was already in Egypt. Then Joseph died, and all his brothers, and all that generation. But the descendants of Israel were fruitful and increased greatly; they multiplied and grew exceedingly strong; so that the land was filled with them.*

Nine score and some-odd years ago our fathers
brought forth upon this stolen continent
another national entity conceived,
so we have all been told, in liberty
and dedicated to the proposition,
so we have all been schooled, that man is man,
one man created equal to another,
and every man—this always was implicit—
to live in freedoms to and freedoms from:
freedom to find and be and rule himself;
freedom from any kind of tyranny
of mind or body, any subtle kind
of thought manipulation, any brand
of native North-American pharaohism.

Maybe it wasn't Egypt at the start—
I mean nine score and some-odd years ago—
since Egypt is another name for bondage,
and we were free.

                    Or that's our recollection.
But can we *know* a past, especially one
that's celebrated, ritualized, and made
a kind of cultic act, its distant smoke
inhaled, refined, through purifying filters?

17

It really wasn't Egypt then—at least
so speaks the ritual myth. The land was free.
But then our Joseph died, our Washington,
our Jefferson, our own staunch patriarchs.
And the descendants of our Israel
were fruitful, multiplied and filled the land.
And we were joined, as Israel was joined,
by some who came to Israel as slaves
and some who came in hope of promised lands.
The land was filled with us. The cities now
were overrun with us. America
the Beautiful becomes the land of Egypt.
   O beautiful for smoggy skies,
     For washing of the brain,
   For hillsides stripped of majesties,
     For strontium in rain.
   Imperial America,
     Thy power preys on thee,
   And damns the good of brotherhood
     From sea to oily sea.

Nine score and some-odd years ago; we think
it really wasn't Egypt then—at least
so speaks the ritual myth: The land was free.
Look, for example, at the campus scene.
The country and the campus then were clean:
John Harvard first in sixteen thirty-six;
William and Mary, sixteen ninety-three;
Old Elihu supplying Yale a name
still years before the birth of Washington.
But then, however true the ritual myth,
however pure and free the origins,
establishments of higher learning, like
the sons of Jacob, grew exceeding strong,
were fruitful, multiplied—and filled the land.

II

Exodus
1:8,
KJV *Now there arose a new king over Egypt,
who knew not Joseph.*

Egypt now is Egypt,
since Egypt is the state of namelessness,
of heedlessness, of human deprivation,
of making man not simply less than God
but less than man in stature, psyche, mind.
Joseph's descendants lose identity
except as his descendants. Persons are
depersonned, losing face by being faceless,
reduced from "thou" to "it," from personhood
to function, category, type, profession,
from separate, total human entity
to functionaries in the national temple.

Even within the university
the single unit, man, was lost. Of course.
The student populations grew from tens
to hundreds, thousands, even tens of thousands.
William and Mary's campus progeny,
like Jacob's sons and daughters, are confined
to purposes defined by Pharaoh's will.

And so, the age-old question sounds again:
Is Pharaoh made for man or man for Pharaoh?
Who serves who's purposes? Who said, "The sabbath
was made for man, not man for sabbath"? Or,
who said, how many times, to all the forms
of Pharaoh—human, institutional,
political—*now let my people go?*

III

Exodus
1:9 ff. *"Look," Pharaoh said to his people, "these people, the sons of Israel, have become so numerous and strong that they are a threat to us. We must be prudent. If war should break out, they might add to the number of our enemies. They might escape out of the country." Accordingly, the Egyptians forced the sons of Israel into slavery, and made their lives unbearable with hard labor, work with clay and with brick, all kinds of work in the fields.*

Stay
with clay.
Stick
to brick.
The system yields
to work in the established fields.
When the boys come out to play
keep your faith in yesterday.
Avoid the whip, eschew the lash,
and don't complain about the hash.
Those who do it Pharaoh's style
will be around for quite a while.

IV

Exodus
3:1 ff. *Now Moses led his flock to Horeb, the mountain of God. And lo, a bush was burning yet it was not consumed. And Moses said, "I will turn aside and see this great sight, why the bush is not burnt." And God called to him from the midst of the bush, "Moses, Moses!" And he said, "Here am I." Then God said, "Put off your shoes from your feet, for the place on which you are standing is holy ground."*

So call us, Moses. Here we are at Horeb.
The Holy Mountain is the Holy Church;
or is it Holy University;
or Holy Home; or Business Enterprise?
Whatever be our private sanctuary,
the Egypt of the world is far-removed
from us. The oppressive ways of Pharaohism
need not disturb us here. Our various priests
in Academe, priests of the God of Learning;
or churchly priests, dispensing full support
for status quo which is our meat and drink;
or priests in Washington, apparently
with access to the oracle of God—
in any case, our priests are able to
defend us from all ills in this bleak world.
Who cares about the next?

And if we live
as good communicants—in Academe
in sober worship of the God who rules
the land of academic discipline,
where one drinks deep from wells of mathematics
and science, engineering, geophysics;
where one digests the proffered, packaged past
of all man's long-accumulated treasures,
of all his stunning, sordid, devious ways;
if in the Church without examination
we take the proffered faith; if in this land
we play the nation's power games with zest—
then great will be the ultimate rewards:
a safe profession, ever larger flocks
and herds, security and private order
in public insecurity and chaos.

V

But what will you do with the bush, my friend,
  O what will you do with the bush?
What do you make of the fire that burns,
  but fails to consume what it burns?
What will you say to the voice that you hear
  from out of the heart of the fire?
What do you answer the Word that calls "Holy"
  the ground of the burning,
  the ground of your standing?
And what do you say to the call out of burning,
  the call out of Egypt,
  the call from the world;
  the call of your brothers,
  the crying of man?

What will you do? That crazy bush is burning.
That Voice is calling, "This is Holy Ground!"
Your place and time are holy; set apart—
but not for refuge from the mortal storm.
If this is what you want, then close your ears,
and turn your back, and walk away.
Refuse to see the bush, deny the Voice,
and shut yourself away from human bondage.

The burning bush, the Voice, the Word, remain.
Look close to see what burns without consumption:
the black man's bitterness is burning; hate
is in the fire, unconsumed; cities
are burning; smugness and hypocrisy,
conformity and apathy still burn;
the noxious gas of all our national jargon
still feeds the fire;
                           and poverty;
                                        and war.

And if we do not turn away, the Voice
and Word are clear out of the burning bush.
our Horeb is accursed if it becomes
in any way at all a sanctuary,
an isolated academic tower,
or pious theological retreat
or fortress held to be impregnable;
if it is deemed to give us special tenure;
if Pharaoh's victims are ignored, if Egypt
is abandoned, . . . and the burning burns.

VI

The burning burns. It isn't Scotland burning.
It's not the city dump. The burning bush,
with inexhaustible supplies of fuel,
is man, incinerating man; mankind,
the corporate species, from the start till now
engaged in what would seem to be a sort
of diabolical self-immolation.
The powerful believe that they survive—
a rank deceit. Their own integrity,
their own humanity, are first to burn;
and what remains makes mockery of man—
a mean, distorted image of creation.

It is some kind of irreducible,
irrefutable gut theology
that puts God in the center of the burning:
"God called to Moses from the middle of the bush."
When will we learn that any Word of God
dissociated from the human scene
is fraudulent? The Word of God in prophet
is always in the midst of human burning;
the Word of God in Christ comes in the heat
of searing tears and burning blood and flesh
of incandescent man. So Christ and prophet,
Word and Voice, the old and new I AM,
are truly heard from in the midst
of all our tortured human conflagrations.

VII

Exodus
3:10 ff. *God said to Moses, "Come, I will send you to Pharaoh that you may bring my people out of Egypt." But Moses said, "Who am I, that I should go?"*

Come off it, Lord. I'm not the man for this.
I like it cool. What kind of fireball God
are you? We've speculated all these years
about your nature; now I think you must
be made of pure, ineffable asbestos.
But what you have to bear in mind is that
your servant here, this guy you take to be
a Moses-type, is really made of stuff
highly combustible. You'll let me say,
again, I like it cool.

                    And furthermore,
I've got it made, since I can make the grade;
and since I have the very best credentials.
You want these days and years at my own Horeb
to point me back into the human fires
that burn around the nation and the world.
Go find someone with less at stake than I,
someone with less to lose. And will you move
your fireball presence somewhere else, or come
away from hiding in that foolish bush?
The Lord be with you, Lord. I'm not your man.
I've got it made. I like to keep it cool.
I'll stay and gather rosebuds while I may,
and cash them in to keep your world at bay.

VIII

You won't take "no"? You say, "I will be there
with you." Ah, there's the rub!

             Now listen, Friend:
I'll tell it like it is. A lot of us
would like to see you die, and some of us
have tried to bury you by declaration.
It isn't for the petty stuff—I mean
the allegations of your beard, your place
in heaven, and all the human attributes
by which you are effectively diminished.
I'm trying to say, I do not really think
we wish you dead because the talk of you,
the human talk of God, so often comes
from stupid men who twist you into forms
of their own prejudice and piety.

Your most intelligent, discerning foes,
your strongest opposition, really come
not now from those who deem your presence here
to be irrelevant, though this they claim.
It is your very relevance, the weight
of your direct impingement on our burning;
it is the overwhelming cost to us
of your excruciatingly direct,
your absolutely relevant, demands.

We do not fault *you* for the fusilade
of petty bullets fired from some quarters
of Christendom, the impotent barrage
of popcorn shot from moralistic guns.
We cannot tolerate the sound of you,
the very name of you, because your name
is justice, love, compassion—qualities
we cannot bring to bear upon our times
without surrendering the cherished ways
that make *us* little gods upon the earth.

I like it here. Don't plague *me* with the plagues
of man and history. I like it here.
I like the perquisites, fringe benefits,
of my own special privilege. I can
avoid the burning bush.
                              And you.
                                    And man.

IX

In Exodus 4—the closing scene of his call—Moses, still resisting, asks in effect to be further persuaded. So Yahweh asks Moses, "What is that in your hand?" "A staff," Moses says. "Throw it on the ground," Yahweh commands; so Moses throws his staff on the ground and it turns into a serpent.

But when, at the command of the Word, he catches it, it becomes a staff again. He is told to put his hand under his clothes against his chest. When he draws it out it is covered with leprosy. At the command of the Word, he repeats the gesture and his hand is restored. Finally, water which he takes from the river turns to blood, when he pours it out on the ground. The saga does not tell us so, but the parallel inference is clear: at the command of the Word, spilled blood can be turned back to fresh water, death can be turned back again to life.

The Word speaks now to Moses and to us:

Look at the ugly miracles of man,
the fabulous magician. See him take
the structures of support, and by his magic
turn them into instruments of death.
His brilliant, twisted alchemy makes sickness
where there was health, disease where human wholeness.
And wonder of all miserable wonders,
this wonder-working fellow has the power
to take life-giving water, flowing, fresh,
and pour it on the ground in blood and death.

We can revise his magic, thou and I.
We can effect the countermiracle.
The venomous, unleashed, can be contained
in structures that support the life of man.
The programmed, calculated brokenness
of man can be restored, his health returned.
And we can turn the tide of death to life.

X

**Exodus
4:10 ff.** Moses said to the Lord, "But, my Lord, never in my life have I been a man of eloquence, either before or since you have spoken to your servant. I am a slow speaker and not able to speak well." "Who gave man his mouth," the Lord answered him. "Who makes him dumb or deaf, gives him sight or leaves him blind? Is it not I? Now go, I shall help you to speak and tell you what to say."

PART 2

THE BURNING
IN THE TEMPLE

Introduction to Isaiah 6

The call of Isaiah took place twenty-seven centuries ago. That prophet had an exceptionally long life and ministry, extending over the reigns of at least four kings of his country, Judah. Isaiah was an urbanite, living in what was for him and his countrymen *the* city, Jerusalem. His language, his politics, and even his theology are impressively shaped by his urban existence.

And he is a man highly placed in Jerusalem, either by virtue of professional status or possibly by royal birth or by both. King Ahaz listens to him, if he does not heed him; and King Hezekiah, by any standard one of Judah's most distinguished kings, not only listens and heeds, but is strongly dependent on Isaiah.

I suppose we would have to say that none of the great Old Testament prophets is typical. Each is so powerfully himself. But no prophet represents classical prophetism more forcefully, more comprehensively, more eloquently, than Isaiah. He is, in the best sense of the word, the most sophisticated of the prophets. But it is finally his own honest, unneurotic, thoroughly realistic appraisal of himself and his own generation together with his historical and existential knowledge of the Word of God in time, Holiness, the Holy One in our midst, that create the essence of Isaiah's distinction.

Verses from Isaiah 6

1 ff. *In the year that King Uzziah died I saw the Lord sitting upon a throne, high and lifted up; and his train filled the temple. Above him stood the seraphim; each had six wings; with two he covered his face, with two he covered his feet, and with two he flew. And one called to another and said: "Holy, holy, holy is the Lord of hosts; the whole earth is full of his glory."*

4 f. *And the foundations of the thresholds shook at the voice of him who called, and the house was filled with smoke.*

[The shaking of foundations, and fire and smoke also elsewhere in the Old Testament signify the presence of God.]

And I said: "Woe is me! For I am lost; for I am a man of unclean lips . . . ; for my eyes have seen the King, the Lord of hosts!"

[Perhaps we should read "the King" in contrast to King Uzziah.]

6 f. *Then flew one of the seraphim to me, having in his hand a burning coal which he had taken with tongs from the altar. And he touched my mouth, and said: "Behold, this has touched your lips; your guilt is taken away, and your sin forgiven."*
[And this is all we know or hear of seraphim. They appear nowhere else in the Old Testament. The Hebrew root has to do with "burning."]

8 ff. *And I heard the voice of the Lord saying, "Whom shall I send, and who will go for us?" Then I said, "Here am I! Send me." And he said, "Go and say to this people:*
[It seems clear in what follows that Isaiah is looking back on the experience of his Call from a point much later in his long ministry when it seems to him that his own prophetic career has served only to make his people more obdurate.]
'Hear and hear, but do not understand;
see and see, but do not perceive.'
Make the heart of this people fat,
and their ears heavy,
and shut their eyes;
lest they see with their eyes,
and hear with their ears,
and understand with their hearts,
and turn and be healed."

11 *Then I said, "How long, O Lord?" And he said:*
"Until cities lie waste
without inhabitant,
and houses without men,
and the land is utterly desolate."

It is Isaiah who speaks first; then the Reverend Doctor Winner; and finally, briefly, Davie Napier.

It is Isaiah speaking now, this month, this year. Not in the year that King Uzziah of Judah died—about 740 B.C. Not twenty-seven hundred years ago. But now.

I

It is the year that King Uzziah died.
That's any year—for kings, my friend, are dying;
since any child of man is child of God,
born to be free, and to subdue the earth.
My God, we go on killing kings like flies;
potential kings, the little kids that perish,
puking away their short-lived animation;
starved or exposed; or caught by rampant wars
imposed by men who would be emperors,
restraining other men from exercising
their given right to live as kings, as men.

35

This is the year—these are the years—when kings
are dying, sacrificed to feed the arrogance
of emperors concerned (they say) to save
(they say) the world (they say) from "commanists"
(they say). And they, these mighty emperors,
will save the world, by God, if saving means
destruction.

          See the year of dying kings,
aborted births of kings, the stillborn kings—
black kings, deprived of crown, and dispossessed
of kingdom.

II

         See the year of emperors
whose law and order function to preserve
the rights of emperors, and to deprive
the rights of kings, the freedom to be men.

The emperors—they come in several colors,
appear in many lands and capitals,
hold office in establishments of law
and labor, commerce, education—
the emperors deprive the kings of kingdom;
make every year a year of kingly death;
suppress the sometimes raucous stuff of freedom,
creative chaos of conflicting kings and kingdoms
in which restless, tumultuous state alone
man can emerge as man, and live as king.

III

It is the year that King Uzziah died.
I see the Lord. Well now, that's stretching things.
No man sees God, for heaven's sake. If God
is God he's not accessible to view
by any kind of pious peeping Tom—
be he prophet or priest or even saint.

If now we talk of sensing Holiness,
if we suspect an unexpected Presence;
if from the lips of seraphim not seen
before or since or, in the normal way
of apprehending, even now, we think
we hear a word of glory in the earth;
if we are sensitive to mystery;
if in the private place of our existence
we freshly sense the possibilities
of life, of new creation, restoration—
we know it has to do with dying kings,
and with our apprehension of the loss
of kingliness.

It is against the fact
of death, the scene of human unfulfillment;
it is against the knowledge of our woe,
the recognition of the sucking vacuum
of all our inhumanity that we,
among the world's sophisticated folk,
have intimations that our world of death,
our place of bleak unholiness, can be
invaded by the glory of the Holy.

This is the year of King Uzziah's death,
and these are times when kingliness is crushed,
when man, conceived to be a little less
than God, is less than man. This is a time
of shaking of foundations—and a time
of burning.

IV

When the kingdom of mankind
is not a kingdom, but for most a prison,
a form of tight, inhibiting restraint
of realization of humanity;
when man's existence, when the very temple
that is his total corporate habitation
is shaken to its deepest understructure,
its long-submerged supports, its cornerstones;
and when his house, this earthly tabernacle,
is filled with smoke of man's incineration—
his burning anger, bitterness, frustration,
his burning hate, humiliation, hunger,
his burning pride, consuming self-concern,
his burning psyche and his burning flesh—
When all of this occurs, and it is now,
it is a time of Calling . . . and a time
of certainty that Holiness is here.

V

Of course, you may deny all this, insist
you do not read this season of our life
this way. You may be one who hears and hears
but does not understand, who sees and sees,
refusing to perceive. You may deny
the shaking of the world's foundations, smoke
from human conflagrations. You may be
an emperor, contemptuous of kings,
of men who would be men. If this is true,
your temple is a miniature illusion,
your sanctuary is a private place
complete with garden for a ghostly walk,
an unreal, insubstantial tête-à-tête
among the dew-kissed roses. You will let me
wish you and your non-Jesus Jesus well.

The time of burning is the time of calling.
The knowledge, the acknowledgment, that man
is reeling in a deeply shaken world
opens the eye and ear to Holiness,
to Glory in the earth. The awful sense
that we are all unclean, immersed in death,
makes possible the vision of the King.

VI

Some see the vision in another way,
Some read this matter very differently.

I yield the floor to Reverend Doctor Winner,
no doubt of Norman stock, invincible.

"What is this talk of death? Isaiah lies.
To be a king, a living king, one has
but to confront oneself with fortitude.
One must resolve to think in positive,
affirmative, American, red-white-
and-blue, noncommunist, nonradical,
[nonbiblical?], autohypnotic terms.

"Isaiah's call should read: It was the year
that King Uzziah died. Poor man, he failed
to use the formula sufficiently.
He failed to tell himself repeatedly,
feet squarely planted, shoulders back, facing
his mirror with a smile, 'Kings never die!'
How should Isaiah's calling read? The year
of fire and death; the shaking of the Temple
of human habitation; burning time
in human history—maybe. But this
is not for me. It is for lesser men.
For I am in Jerusalem a man
of privilege, admired, accepted, loved;
a man of parts, acquainted with the ways
of royalty. As one to whom men turn
in hope, I am upheld in high esteem.

"Why should I bear the griefs and carry sorrows
of other men? Why let myself be hurt?
Why carry wounds of other men's transgressions;
and why be bruised for their iniquities?

"Or why, indeed, be called? I'll be the Caller!
Let other men protest of unclean lips
and take for cure the purifying fire.
I'm not about to be an errand boy
of Holiness!

"It is the year of death
and I resolve that with the help of me,
myself, and my resources, I will live.
I will believe in me, myself, and so
should you. Now, suddenly, I see myself
upon a lofty throne. I know my strength.
I stamp upon my mind indelibly
the vivid image of my own success.
And it is I who say, 'Who now will go
for us?' and God responds, 'I'm here. Use me.'"

VII

So runs the version of the call revised
by Doctor Winner, and cordially endorsed
by clean, white, Anglo-Saxon Protestants
who think they have it made, or want to think
they have it made, by virtue of their own,
their very private merit; who believe
that God who knows a good thing when he sees it
is standing by them ready to respond,
and make of any untoward situation
an instant Camelot—for them, of course,
and other knights and ladies of the faith.

VIII

These are the awful days of dying kings,
when men, born to be men, are less than men.
The sacrificial altar fire is burning.
Foundations shake. And we are all unclean.
But if we listen with prophetic ears,
within the smoke-filled temple of our world
the seraphim are calling, burning calls
to burning, strangely not of death but life,
not of despair, but hope, and not of shame
but glory. Burning cries of holiness,
invading all of man's unholiness,
as Christ, the son of God, the son of man,
the king—unceasingly invading time,
incessantly enduring crucifixion—
proclaims the ultimate but, in a sense,
already present rule of righteousness.

IX

If you are burned by burning, intimate
with altar fires; if your own lips are seared
with burning coals from sacrificial altars;
if crucifixion—once for all in Christ
or in the bloody stream of human history—
if crucifixion of the son of man
fully impinges on your consciousness,
then you will not be able to escape
the Calling of the Caller; you will know
that you are called, called irresistibly,
without a word of promise of success;
called out against insuperable odds
to go and speak and work and live, in faith
that judgment must be finally redemptive,
that fire ultimately purifies,
that burning is for cleansing and forgiveness,
that love and righteousness and holiness
in fact pervade this shattered habitation.

And you and I are called to live in love
and affirmation of a burning world,
in confidence that corporate guilt is purged,
our corporate want of cleanness is forgiven;
that even if the smoke is never cleared
a Holiness invades our wanton violence
and Glory fills the anguish of our times.

X

The year that King Uzziah died: a time
of burning, time of shaking, time of calling.
"Whom shall I send and who will go for us?"
And I say, trembling like a slender reed
before the hurricane, in hope alone
of love and affirmation, confidence—
I say, "I think I'm here. Send me."

PART 3

THE BURNING
IN THE BONES

Verses from Jeremiah 1, 20, and 8

1:1 f. *The words of Jeremiah, the son of Hilkiah, of the priests who were in Anathoth in the land of Benjamin, to whom the word of the Lord came in the days of Josiah the son of Amon, king of Judah:*

1:5–8 *"Before I formed you in the womb I knew you, and before you were born I consecrated you; I appointed you a prophet to the nations." Then I said, "Ah, Lord God! Behold, I do not know how to speak, for I am only a youth." But the Lord said to me,*
> *"Do not say, 'I am only a youth';*
> *for to all to whom I send you you shall go,*
> *and whatever I command you you shall speak.*
> *Be not afraid of them,*
> *for I am with you to deliver you."*

1:9 f. *Then the Lord put forth his hand and touched my mouth; and the Lord said to me,*
> *"Behold, I have put my words in your mouth.*
> *See, I have set you this day over nations*
>   *and over kingdoms*
> *to pluck up and to break down,*
> *to destroy and to overthrow,*
> *to build and to plant."*

20:7-9 O Lord, thou hast deceived me, and I was deceived;
thou art stronger than I, and thou hast prevailed.
I have become a laughingstock all the day . . . ;
For whenever I speak, I cry out,
I shout, "Violence and destruction!"
For the word of the Lord has become for me
a reproach and derision all day long.
If I say, "I will not mention him,
or speak any more in his name,"
there is in my heart as it were a burning fire
shut up in my bones,
and I am weary with holding it in,
and I cannot.

8:18 f. My grief is beyond healing, my heart is sick within me.
Hark, the cry of the daughter of my people
from the length and breadth of the land:

8:20-22 "The harvest is past, the summer is ended,
and we are not saved."
For the wound of the daughter of my people
is my heart wounded,
I mourn, and dismay has taken hold on me.
Is there no balm in Gilead?
Is there no physician there?
Why then has the health of the daughter of my people
not been restored?

I

Suppose we play the role of Jeremiah.
Suppose we take his part, assume his stance,
appropriate his point of view. Our world
becomes his world, our time and people his.

And we are Jeremiah, called by God
or Yahweh, called by Zeus or Allah, called
by unseen Spirit, Voice, or Word of Him
who was and is and evermore shall be;
the Source and Sustenance of life and love;
Existence that is nonexistent—THOU
the Inescapable, in every "I"
and "you" and "he" and "we" and "they."

II

So we
are Jeremiah. More than most, we are
gregarious, and more than most we know
the longing to be heard, accepted, loved.
Intensely *people* people, we would like
to speak the sparkling, pleasing word,
the soothing word, the word of confidence,
the undisturbing word, the word of praise
for sacred things like life and liberty
and the pursuit of happiness; and truth
of course; America the beautiful;
in God we trust, and in the Pentagon,
Apollo, Saturn, Jupiter, and Mars;
and Jesus saves the democratic way
of life and every day in every way
grow old along with me because the best
is surely yet to be in this fair land
possessed by people who are brave and free.

III

Like any other man, we want success
as measured by the instruments devised
by those who have achieved success. We want
to move into the councils of the mighty.
We know the royal things, the royal way
to royal places of security.
We're bright enough to learn the rules and play
the game and win. One exercises tact,
of course. Sequential choices must be made
discriminately, shall we say. One picks
one's schools, one's friends, profession, even spouse,
not for themselves alone but for their worth,
their calculated value, in the game.
If money is the game, don't hesitate
to take it anywhere from anyone.
But privately, select prestigious forms
of recreation with prestigious folk.
As J. P. Morgan put it once,
"You do your business thing with anyone,
your sailing only with a gentleman."

We know the game, the way to privilege.
We know the road that winds from Anathoth
up to the summit of Jerusalem;
from Anaheim to Nob Hill, San Francisco.
We understand who rules, and how and why,
and where they congregate—the royal haunts,
Mount Desert, Martha's Vineyard, Harbor Point;
the royal clubs, Bohemian and Links,
Pacific Union, Century Club, Duquesne,
Chicago, Philadelphia; and Yale,
and Stanford, Harvard, Princeton, and the rest.

We know the way to get oneself inside
the power structure of Jerusalem.
Or Babylon. And we would take the way.

IV

I, Jeremiah, want the royal way,

But there's a burning in my bones
and there's a fire in my heart
and hate is loose to tear apart
the work man loves, the love he owns.

I, Jeremiah, want the way,
But every time I draw my breath
to speak, I shout, "Destruction, death!"
And I am taken with dismay.

I could be silent like the stones
or learn to play a quieter part;
but there's a fire in my heart,
and there's a burning in my bones.

V

The burning burns, and we are driven men,
possessed, seduced—by What, by God, by Christ,
by some infernal THOU stronger than we.
It is as if we never had the choice,
as if this burning THOU had staked his claim
not now, nor in some yesterday, nor yet
within the embryo. The seeds of burning
were planted as if it were before the sperm:
"Before I formed you in the womb, I knew you!"

By God, you make us all some kind of Christ!
And that's no bloody way to be a man,
deprived of freedom to be free, compelled
to speak the Word men will not hear
at home in Anathoth or anywhere—
the Word of plucking up and breaking down,
the dreaded Word of violence and destruction.

VI

The burning burns inside, within my bones.
The burning Word must out. The present course
of man is suicide. If white men now,
at last, do not at once open for blacks
the power levels they have long maintained;
if men who *have* continue to withhold
from men who are deprived of what they have;
if men who put their highest trust in flags
cannot now own a higher loyalty;
if educated men will not with grace
make theirs a privilege accessible
to human categories long deprived;
if in our monstrous, heedless, headlong greed
we worship clever *things* our hands have made;
if we persist in making waters sick,
our air the septic tank of locomotion—
that mechanistic, technological,
swift-moving, diarrheal trafficking
on land and sea and air; if we permit
our earth, the mother of our milk and bread,

to be or to become a poison waste;
if we by lust or passion, pride or fear,
if we, by theological perversion,
produce in mounting flow increasing hordes
of humankind; if man cannot at last
be man, subdue the earth, subdue himself
and his own passions, live with love and justice . . .
Then, God, how burns the burning in my bones,
and I must cry of violence and destruction.

Old Jeremiah called it judgment. We,
the younger Jeremiahs of our day
may call it what we will; but it is death.

The burning shut up in our weary bones;
the fire that burns internally; the Word,
the scorching Word, that cannot be restrained
is consciousness of doom—the certain sense
that if we cannot live as men with men
we cannot live at all.

VII

If we could hear
as Jeremiah heard, if the raw Word
of Yahweh could break in, break through to us,
what would we hear? Suppose, let's just suppose
that vast facade, our tranquil Western front,
the heavy structure of our intellect,
were penetrated by the Word. Suppose
that hard, inhibiting, thick overlay
of conscious mind long since surrendered to
parochial notions of reality
were pierced to leave exposed responsive depths
of mind that otherwise lie locked and frozen
beneath our stubborn surface consciousness.
Suppose we heard for once the Very Voice.
What might it say to this-day's Jeremiahs?

YAHWEH: Davie! You talk too much. What are you doing up there in a black bathrobe? Who are all those people out there? Never mind. They look very clean . . . very decent . . . very square. Where are the beards? I always liked beards. The prophets, you know. And of course there was my son . . .

Well, enough of this. We haven't got all day. The stubborn surface consciousness will be closing over again to become once more that hard, inhibiting, thick overlay of conscious mind—I believe those were your words . . .

BDN: Yes, Lord.

YAHWEH: In any case, we do not want to exceed twenty minutes for this part of the service. (Pause) You sometimes do, you know.

BDN: Yes, Lord.

YAHWEH: The last time around, you pushed it very close.

BDN: Yes, Lord. Forgive me, Lord.

YAHWEH: That's good. Now what are we doing today? Oh, yes. I know. Are you ready? Davie, Davie, put off your shoes from off your feet, for the place on which you are standing is holy ground . . .

BDN (*interrupting*): No, Lord. Excuse me, Sir. That's Moses. We did the Burning Bush. We're working with Jeremiah today.

YAHWEH: You want me to begin, then—Before I formed you in the womb, I knew you.

BDN: That's it.

YAHWEH: And you want the Jeremiah word for now, in your language?

BDN: Yes, Lord.

YAHWEH: Are you ready?

BDN: Yes, Lord.

There's something happening here
What it is ain't exactly clear.
There's a man with a gun over there
Telling me I got to beware.
   Think it's time we stop . . . children, what's that sound,
   Everybody look what's going down.

There's battle lines being drawn
Nobody's right if everybody's wrong
Young people speaking their minds
Getting so much resistance from behind
   It's time we stop, hey, what's that sound,
   Everybody look what's going down.

What a field day for the heat
A thousand people in the street
Singing songs and a-carrying signs
Mostly say hurrah for our side.
It's time we stop, hey, what's that sound,
Everybody look what's going down.

Paranoia strikes deep
Into your life it will creep
It starts when you're always afraid,
Step outa line the man come and take
you away.

We better stop, hey, what's that sound
Everybody look what's going
We better stop, hey, what's that sound,
Everybody look what's going
We better stop, hey, what's that sound.
Everybody look what's going
Stop, children, what's that sound
Everybody look what's goin' . . . .

YAHWEH: Davie!
BDN: Yes, Lord.

YAHWEH: Are you there?

BDN: Yes, Lord. The important question is, Are *you*?

YAHWEH: I AM. I WILL BE. I CAUSE TO BE. So what you have said, and what I have said, and what we have heard— this is only one side of Now-Jeremiah, of Jeremiah-Now. For the other side, read from Jeremiah. You know what to read.

> The burning in his bones, the fire, the Word
> that could not be suppressed was doom *and hope,*
> and death *and life;* destroy and overthrow,
> but also build and plant. Read Jeremiah:
> everyman can make his own translation.

And love and faith and hope be with you all.

VIII

Here are lines of hope from Jeremiah as written in the new Roman Catholic Translation, the Jerusalem Bible. Make your own rendering into our present, our immediate now. Make his calling and commission, and his hope your own . . .

"Come back—it is Yahweh who speaks—
I shall frown on you no more,
since I am merciful—it is Yahweh who speaks.
I shall not keep my resentment forever.
Only acknowledge your guilt . . .
and I will give you shepherds after my own heart,
and [they] shall feed you [with] knowledge and [understanding]   (3:12–13a, 15, JB)."

See, the days are coming—it is Yahweh who speaks—when I am going to sow . . . and as I once watched [over men] to tear up, to break down, to overthrow, destroy and bring disaster, so now I shall watch over them to build and to plant. It is Yahweh who speaks   (31:27 f., JB).

"Go now to those to whom I send you
and say whatever I command you. . . .
There! I am putting my words into your mouth . . .
to build and to plant (1:7, 9, 10, JB)."

It is Yahweh who speaks. And now, again, it is Jeremiah who
speaks. *If I say, "I will not mention [Yahweh] or speak any*
more in his name," there is in my heart as it were a burning
fire shut up in my bones, and I am weary with holding it
in, and I cannot (20:9).

IX

The burning shut up in our weary bones;
the fire that burns internally; the Word,
incendiary Word that cannot be restrained,
is in itself a paradox: it is
at once the anguish of our corporate drive
for death and, quite in equal strength, the knowledge
that we are men, children of God, beloved
of him, and ultimately loved enough
to know that love portrayed in terms of Christ;
that we are men, ourselves quite capable
of that same love by which we are beloved.

And given consciousness of that one Word
transcending other words, the paradox
of burning in our bones embracing dark
and light, despair and hope, will in the end
find resolution in the world's redemption
from man's obsession with the ways of death.

X

Hush; listen; soft. I hear his groans—
man beating man, life torn apart.
But there's a fire in my heart,
and there's a burning in my bones.

PART 4

THE BURNING
IN GOD AND MAN

Verses from Jonah and the Gospels

**Jonah
1:1 ff.** Now the word of the Lord came to Jonah the son of Amittai, saying, "Arise, go to Nineveh, that great city, and cry against it; for their wickedness has come up before me." But Jonah . . . went down to Joppa and found a ship going to Tarshish . . . away from the presence of the Lord.

1:4 f. But the Lord hurled a great wind upon the sea, and there was a mighty tempest on the sea, so that the ship threatened to break up. Then the mariners were afraid.

1:7 And they said to one another, "Come, let us cast lots, that we may know on whose account this evil has come upon us." So they cast lots, and the lot fell upon Jonah.

1:11 f. Then they said to him, "What shall we do to you, that the sea may quiet down for us?" For the sea grew more and more tempestuous. He said to them, "Take me up and throw me into the sea; then the sea will quiet down for you; for I know that it is because of me that this great tempest has come upon you."

1:15 *So they took up Jonah and threw him into the sea; and the sea ceased from its raging.*

1:17 *And the Lord appointed a great fish to swallow up Jonah; and Jonah was in the belly of the fish three days and three nights.*

2:10 *[Then] the Lord spoke to the fish, and it vomited out Jonah upon the dry land.*

3:1 ff. *Then the word of the Lord came to Jonah the second time, saying, "Arise, go to Nineveh, that great city, and proclaim to it the message that I tell you." So Jonah arose and went to Nineveh . . . and cried, "Yet forty days, and Nineveh shall be overthrown!"*

4:5 *Then Jonah went out of the city and sat to the east of the city, and made a booth for himself there. He sat under it in the shade, till he should see what would become of the city.*

3:5 ff. *And the people of Nineveh believed God; they proclaimed*
(Cf. Joel *a fast, and put on sackcloth, from the greatest of them to*
1:13 f.) *the least of them. Then . . . the king . . . made proclamation*
and published through Nineveh, "By the decree of the king
and his nobles: Let . . . everyone turn from his evil way
and from the violence which is in his hands. Who knows,
God may yet repent and turn from his [burning] anger, so
(Cf. Joel *that we perish not." When God saw what they did, how they*
2:14) *turned from their evil way, God repented of the evil which*
he had said he would do to them; and he did not do it.

4:1 ff. *But it displeased Jonah exceedingly, and he was [burned up].*
And he . . . said, "I pray thee, Lord, is not this what I said
when I was yet in my country? That is why I made haste
(Cf. Joel *to flee to Tarshish; for I knew that thou art a gracious God*
2:13) *and merciful, slow to anger, and abounding in steadfast love,*
and repentest of evil. Therefore, now, O Lord, take my life
from me, I beseech thee, for it is better for me to die than
to live." And the Lord said, "Do you do well to be [burned
up]?"

4:6 ff. [Then] the Lord God appointed a plant, and made it come up over Jonah, that it might be a shade over his head, to save him from his discomfort. So Jonah was exceedingly glad because of the plant. But when dawn came up the next day, God appointed a worm which attacked the plant, so that it withered. When the sun rose, God appointed a sultry east wind, and the sun beat upon the head of Jonah so that he was faint; and he asked that he might die, and said, "It is better for me to die than to live." But God said to Jonah, "Do you do well to [burn with anger over] the plant?" And he said, "I do well to be [burned up, even] enough to die." And the Lord said, "You pity the plant, for which you did not labor, nor did you make it grow, which came into being in a night, and perished in a night. And should not I pity Nineveh, that great city, in which there are more than a hundred and twenty thousand persons who do not know their right hand from their left, and also much cattle?"

Mark 8:11–13, NEB Then the Pharisees came out and engaged Jesus in discussion. To test him they asked him for a sign from heaven. He sighed deeply to himself and said, "Why does this generation ask for a sign? I tell you this: no sign shall be given to this generation." With that he left them, re-embarked, and went off to the other side of the lake.

Matthew 16:1–4, NEB The Pharisees and Sadducees came, and to test him they asked him to show them a sign from heaven. His answer was: "It is a wicked generation that asks for a sign; and the only sign that will be given it is the sign of Jonah." So he went off and left them.

Luke 11:29–30, 32, NEB With the crowds swarming round him he went on to say: "This is a wicked generation. It demands a sign, and the only sign that will be given to it is the sign of Jonah. For just as Jonah was a sign to the Ninevites, so will the Son of Man be to this generation. . . . The men of Nineveh will appear at the judgment when the men of this generation are on trial, and ensure their condemnation, for they repented at the preaching of Jonah; and what is here is greater than Jonah.

Now once upon a time the Word of Yahweh
confronted Jonah, son of Amittai:
"Arise and go to Nineveh, the city,
the capital of great Assyria,
and cry against it—for their wickedness
is great enough to come before my face."

I

It happened once upon a time; that is,
it never was but always is. It happens.
It happens in the way of happenings
in parables related in the Gospels;
the way of Salinger and Lewis Carroll;
the way *Of Mice and Men* and *Moby Dick,*
Wind in the Willows, Yellow Submarine;
the way of Ionesco, Tolkien, Milne.

The likes of Cyrus and Napoleon
are once, not once upon an any time.
But sons who spend their substance riotously,
and men who sail beneath a sea of green,
content to live in sweet oblivion;
the Holden Caulfields, Lennies, Bandersnatches,
and whales, rhinoceri, and Alices;
the Hobbits and the Toads and Pooh and Piglet—
these never were but somehow always are.

II

So once upon a very present time,
maybe today, tomorrow, yesterday,
the Word of Yahweh comes to Johnny Jonah,
the son of Amittai or Mr. Jones:
"Arise—this is to say, get off your duff,
your cozy status in Jerusalem,
and get yourself to Nineveh, the place,
it's any place, where life is less than life,
men less than men, where light is turned to dark,
joy into mourning, peace to bloody war,
where ways of death absorb the wealth and mind
of all the living.

                  "Go to Nineveh,
the secular metropolis, the crown
at once of genius and stupidity,
the incestuous cave, colossal smoke-filled room,
the bloody bastion of brutality,
the putrid citadel of violence.

"Get you to Nineveh: get with it, son.
Go where the action is, man against man:
dehumanizing action, hostile, hard.
Go where it is, the city of the world,
whose waters of compassion are polluted,
whose quality of mercy is restrained,
whose store of love long since has been depleted.

"For God's sake go to Nineveh and see—
and tell it like it is. The hour is late,
the judgment imminent, the holocaust
impending now. This is the Word of Yahweh:
My anger and frustration burn; and when
I burn, man burns.

                              "The way to Nineveh?
It has to do not necessarily
with roads and countries, seas and continents;
it has to do with seeing, understanding;
it has to do with knowing what it is
to be a man, and passionately hating
whatever leaves him anywhere unmanned.

"For Christ's sake, go, or come, to Nineveh!"

III

Now Johnny Jonah, listening, speaks up:
"I heard all that. My God, how Yahweh blows!
He's got a lot of wind, and that's a fact.
A funny thing: you know, one possible
interpretation of his name, Yahweh,
connects it with a Hebrew root 'to blow.'
Now isn't that a gas? And here he is,
old Yahweh Zebaoth, the Lord of Hosts,
ranting and raving over Nineveh
as if it were the bloody world gone mad.
'Tell Nineveh of judgment and proclaim
its doom,' he says. 'My anger is on fire:
the men of Nineveh are soon to burn.'

"Well talk about non sequiturs—there's one
to take the prize. He's burning, so man burns.
Old Yahweh blows about his burning wrath,
as if his burning puts in jeopardy
the whole cock-eyed inflammable creation!

"That's great, the Lord of Hosts,
Old Yahweh Zebaoth—
Much better, Lord of Boasts,
Old Yahweh Billy Goat!

"So blow, old Blower, blow;
And burn, old Burner, burn.
I'm not about to go
Give Nineveh a turn.

"I think I know your mark.
I think I read you right.
You've got an awful bark
For such a gentle bite.

"In anger you are slow,
In steadfast love replete;
So blow, old Blower, blow,
And bleat, old Bleater, bleat."

IV

"I'll call his bluff. I'm not for Nineveh.
The people there are deaf. The die is cast
in Nineveh: the billions go to space,
to ABM deployment, chemical
and biological research for War.
The men of Nineveh are all enslaved
to what they call, O monstrous euphemism,
'defense'—the science and technology
of violence, destruction, and of death—
the while the weightier matters of defense,
of true defense, of justice, mercy, faith,
are tragically neglected.

                              "I am not
for Nineveh. They won't repent. Oh, sure,
they may put on a show, affect a change
of heart, pretend that they are now in fact
committed to the ways of righteousness.
And Yahweh, patient Lover-boy of man,
who loves the world of man enough to give
his life—this is the sense of God in Christ—
Yahweh will once again give amnesty,
which is of course his way ad nauseum.
He will declare the judgment of his wrath—
which never would have fallen anyway—
to be suspended, utterly removed,
annulled.

"And he will talk of faith in man,
belief in man, in Nineveh. 'You care,'
he'll say to me, 'you care for objects, things,
inanimate, impermanent, and as
compared to human values, human life,
quite without worth. You are committed, man,
to things which, so to speak, contrive to thwart,
and insulate against, the awful, hectic heat
of this existence. I, my child—
the Holy One among you, in your midst—
I care for man, for human life;
I care for man's creation, his renewal.
With everlasting, infinite compassion,
I care for man's fulfillment!'

                    "So he'll say.
How laudable of God—or how naïve!—
to hold mankind in faith and hope and love.

"Why is it Yahweh has to pick on me?
I'd like to stay in old Jerusalem,
believing as I do that God, of course,
is packaged in the temple of our faith,
that our concerns are necessarily
identified with his and his with ours.
It burns me up to think that Nineveh
has any claim on Yahweh, let alone
on me. I say, to hell with Nineveh!
No Nineveh for me, my Loving Friend:
I'm off for Tarshish. Tarshish, anyone?"

V

"Now let me tell you. Tarshish is a trip,
an absolutely never-never land—
unqualified *illusion* of escape
from Nineveh, or from Jerusalem;
the always insubstantial *fantasy*
of flight from burning God and burning man.
The trip is hell—it's hell to try to go
to Tarshish. God, I wish I'd headed straight
for Nineveh.

                              "Three days in hell it was.
The writer Aldous Huxley penned some lines
on my unfortunate incarceration.
But he romanticized, he pietized
the whole incredible experience.
With tongue in cheek, of course, he put it so:

'Seated upon the convex mount of one vast kidney,
Jonah prays, and sings his canticles and hymns,
Making the hollow vault resound God's goodness
                              and mysterious ways,
Till the great fish spouts music as he swims.'

"That really isn't how it is at all.
We Johnny Jonah's aren't disposed to sing
when we are caught by Yahweh in a fish
somewhere between Tarshish and Nineveh.
No one rejoices when he finds himself
restrained from breaking loose, brought back again
to face some kind of crucifixion.

                              Look
at Jesus' anguish in Gethsemane."

VI

"My name is Johnny Jonah. I am one
who never was but always am—always
in search of Tarshish; always brought again
to Nineveh; and never satisfied.
If Yahweh burns in anger at the ways
of men in anybody's Nineveh,
he cools it when he sees a sign of hope.
And I, who have proclaimed his wrath, am left
holding the bag. No wonder that I burn!

"Confound you, Yahweh, for a fickle God!
You sensitize me to the awful ways
of men in Nineveh, and make of me
a prophet belching fire and preaching doom
on all who manufacture or contrive
devices of destruction, perpetrate
the fraudulent, support inequity,
and reinforce the old injustices.
And then, my God, you tell me in effect
that these rank fellows claim your hope and love.
It isn't any wonder that I burn!"

VII

So there he goes, the everlastingly
contemporary Jonah, wanting out
from Nineveh, frustrated in his flight
to Tarshish, in a manner crucified
and buried; brought again to life and light;
then mightily condemning Nineveh
for wickedness, and God for being God;
and finally in burning rage protesting
the hope and love of God for Nineveh
and saying in effect, "Burn them, not me!"

A life, a crucifixion, burial—
and then a fully human resurrection
which nonetheless proclaims the love of God
for man, the always openness of life
to new beginnings, fresh and new creation;
the readiness, the eagerness of God
to free men from the bondage of the past
and set them on their way to being men.

VIII

And here we are in our own generation.
Confronted by another life and death
and resurrection. Jesus *was*, of course,
as Jonah never was. But Jesus *is*,
as Jonah is, beyond facticity,
affirming what is true with or without
specific, literal, concrete enactment.
The man who will insist that Jonah's fish
and Jonah's three-day residence therein
are stuff of fact is no more off the mark
than one who wants to stake his Christian faith—
and bind all other men as well thereto—
on flesh and blood and bone facticity
of the post-resurrection animation
of Jesus' body. At its best, that is
to play the role of Pharisee, to seek
a sign, to say, "Show us a miracle
and we'll believe. Make with the magic, Lord,
defy the natural law. Give us a sign from heaven!"

But this was he who said with hurt and heat,
"Why does this generation ask for signs?
I tell you this: no sign is given you
except the sign of Jonah," by which
he meant, no miracle except the Word,
the proclamation of the word of truth,
the word of God, the word of liberty
to be at once the sons of men and God.

IX

The resurrection is. Unless it *is*
it never was, and if it is, it is
in faith, as from the first it was in faith.

And this is after all no Jonah. This
is Jesus Christ. This is the resurrection
of one who is at once the son of God
and son of man.

        And if he *is* for us
then we will know that he is risen now,
that all the sons of men and God are brought
up from the grave of hatred, poverty,
destruction, hunger, impotence, and war;
that death, and all the ways of making death,
can never win; that God himself has staked
his own eternal life upon the premise
not necessarily that man will live
as son of man and God—but that he can!
The inhabitants of Nineveh are loved
with ultimate and everlasting love.

X

It is a time of burning, crucifixion:
It is a time of calling, resurrection.
The calling is to turning, change of heart,
repentance for our corporate ways of death.
The calling calls of human amnesty,
annullment of the past, rebirth, renewal.
It calls to everyone in Nineveh
that all the ways of burning, all the forms
of crucifixion may be wiped away.

The time of burning is a time of calling,
a call to sharing in the resurrection—
authentic reassurance that the ways
of death, the subtle, violent, myriad ways,
can be transformed to ways of life, and man
restored to status as the son of God.